TAKING NOTES

poems by

Beth Kress

Finishing Line Press
Georgetown, Kentucky

TAKING NOTES

Copyright © 2020 by Beth Kress
ISBN 978-1-64662-337-2 First Edition
All rights reserved under International and Pan-American Copyright Conventions. No part of this book may be reproduced in any manner whatsoever without written permission from the publisher, except in the case of brief quotations embodied in critical articles and reviews.

ACKNOWLEDGMENTS

The author gratefully acknowledges the journals in which these poems first appeared:

Avalon Literary Review: "Wandering the Halls"
Dreamers: "The Body as Poem"
Snowy Egret: "Low Tide"
Spotlight: "What's Left" and "Clothesline"
Willow Review: "Afterthought"

I wish to thank all the exceptional people who have inspired me and have graciously encouraged my words, especially Peter McLoughlin. I dedicate this book to them.

Publisher: Leah Huete de Maines
Editor: Christen Kincaid
Cover Art: by artant (from Getty Images)
Author Photo: Peter McLoughlin
Cover Design: Elizabeth Maines McCleavy

Order online: www.finishinglinepress.com
also available on amazon.com

Author inquiries and mail orders:
Finishing Line Press
P. O. Box 1626
Georgetown, Kentucky 40324
U. S. A.

Table of Contents

Where I'm From 1
And So It Begins 2
The Trunk 3
Midnight in Freedom Wisconsin 4
Ten Thousand Miles 5
The Builder 6
Daily Bread 7
Accidental Gift 8
The Body as Poem 9
By the Sea 10
First Hours 11
On Simonton Road 12
Clothesline 13
Afterthought 14
Low Tide 15
After All 16
Stitching 17
The Thread 18
Going Down 19
Seeking 20
Nahant 21
Biking 22
At the French Bakery 23
Wandering the Halls 24
The 4 A.M. Shift with Georgia 25
Kinship 26
What I Brought to Provincetown 27
What's Left 28
Sniper Alley 29
Rounding the Bend 30
Not Sure Why 31
Close Encounters 32
Why I Write 33

Where I'm From

I am from Ireland, England and Germany, Illinois cornfields
and Wisconsin dairy farms, bone-hard winters and healing summers
near the immense shadow of Lake Michigan.

I am from cattle farmers and garment workers
teachers and machinists, railroad switchmen
and homemakers, blacksmiths and secretaries.

I am from plaid uniforms and home-sewn Sunday clothes,
socks darned with cotton thread over a smooth wooden egg,
from dodging the dreaded boxelder bug by day
and falling asleep to a chorus of crickets.

I'm from standing on my friend's back stoop to call out a two-syllable
song of her name—the first note high, the second low–and wait
for the slap of the screen door as she comes blasting out to play.

I'm from rickety bikes for whizzing down hills
and books for reading and re-reading
from mulberry trees to shimmy up and creeks to leap across,
silos filled to bursting and clackety trains carting wheat and corn.

I am from the grit to survive the lonely frontier, tend animals
in blizzards, and guide a plow all day over furrowed fields,
from droughts, dust storms and wilting heat waves.

I am from days when women might not survive childbirth
or children smallpox and fever. I am from the leap of faith
to coax life from the parched earth, the miracle of harvest.

I am from endurance and passion.
I am from sweat and sorrow.
I am from the heartland.

And So It Begins

Have you ever tried to trace
the exact moment
a thing actually begins?
It's usually impossible.

But I do remember once watching
a brown-eyed flower girl
standing in a church vestibule
biting her lip
as she peered down at her new Mary Janes
and I thought about how all the power of time
was in that one tiny tentative foot
when she finally extended it
onto the long swath of white carpet,
bringing a young woman
to the beginning
of a whole new story.

And last October
a half dozen leaves did spiral down
and land on the front steps
like the crisp, coppery whispers
of an ad hoc committee
delivering a message.

The Trunk
for my great- great grandparents

They're speechless on the buggy ride from Essex
after so much weeping, the wrenching farewells.
A slate day—clouds overhead, mud below
a chill creeping in under the lap blanket
every bump in the road to London an accusation,
a dent in the plan.

They'd married in secret against the wishes of her parents
who wanted her to stay in England
and only learned of the wedding two weeks later.
It is 1855. They are on their way to America.
She is now Mrs. Frederick DiVall
no longer the singular Mary Farncombe.

She scans his face for reassurance but he too is lost
studying the passing countryside as if to memorize.
She turns to glance back—her old self is receding.
She catches sight of her trunk strapped on the back, swaying.
Her hand moves to her throat.

Ahead of them a six-week stretch of roiling seas
churning stomachs and a thousand-mile wagon trek
across the rutted, muddy frontier.

When she finally starts to unpack in a small Wisconsin log cabin
she'll hear a wolf howl, stop to look up, then feel something
tucked into the bottom of her trunk: a small packet—
baby clothes stitched by her mother, miniature muslin shirts
that will one day be worn by the ten grandchildren
that soul-sad seamstress will never meet.

Midnight in Freedom Wisconsin

I open the small wooden box that graces
my kitchen counter, seeking no attention.
At home anywhere, it's moved with me a dozen times.
It holds handwritten notes, smudged and splotched
from cooks sweet and salty I've deemed keepers.

It speaks of meals shared,
the tried and the true
of Kaye's Chicken Divan
Peggy Minor's Corn Relish Salad
Nana's Nut Bread, Jim's Ragu Sauce
Aunt Bette's Oven Omelette
and Mom's Lazy Daisy Cake.

It speaks of Cornelius O' Keefe, hunched over
his workbench one midnight in Freedom Wisconsin
holding a half-inch brass hinge between his thumb
and forefinger, attaching it to a small dovetailed box
with sides so thin and so fine they could splinter.
He draws on skills from his Cork youth
to create this gift for his daughter Elizabeth.
She is to be married on this day in 1917.
She is to be my grandmother.

I start to measure and stir and remember
the hands of Cornelius holding this box
up to the light a hundred years ago
the hands of cooks wiping palms on aprons
to write these cards
and bakers, full of warmth and sourdough
dusting off their flour-coated hands
across the decades.

Ten Thousand Miles
for my parents

She'd be wearing the same plaid skirt that swirled
as she raced down the dorm stairs for that first date
(*I fell for her like a ton of bricks*), her knock-out smile,
and her fluffy gray coat. *You look like a million bucks,*
he'd exclaimed, clasping his hands.
He lay on a narrow barracks cot in the sweltering
New Guinea jungle imagining this reunion,
dreaming nightly of her face, her scent, the way she moved.

He tried to picture her pregnant self, and the child.
The due date had come and gone, two weeks without a word.
He'd been a wreck. Then finally, a telegram:
son born November 4, mother/ child well.
In December she'd sent slivers of crescent moons,
first nail clippings. He'd held them in his palm.

He'd navigated a bomber over the South Pacific
with stars and sweaty prayers his only guides.
He could have been dead by now from any one of 39
combat missions and a risky rescue when he was certain
it was over. No. He thought he'd never live to see this day.

Now after ten long months gone, he is stateside at last
on an endless train ride from Frisco to Chicago, inching closer
to the dream of her, of holding his four-month old son.
As the train crawls ever-so-slowly into Union Station
he leans into the window, scanning the platform for her shape,
bodies blocking his view. It is Valentine's Day, 1945.
He is 22 years old. After several heart-thudding minutes
he spots her, standing alone, her small form angled toward him
holding something close to her chest.

The Builder

Take me back to my father
in the side yard of our house on Charles Street
wielding his wheelbarrow around stacks of bricks,
piles of sand and sacks of cement, building a room for us.

Let me stand by his side again
in my denim pedal-pushers and navy blue Keds,
let me watch him feed the mouth
of the crusty old mixer as it rumbles along.

He adds puffs of cement powder, gravel and sand,
his shovel slicing into the mounds again and again,
dousing it all with the garden hose—
Dad, how do you know how much?—
then the swish-tumble as the contents
cascade into the wheelbarrow.

Oh, the joy of being trusted to carry bricks to his side!
As soon as I can build a tall stack, I sit on my heels,
hug my knees and watch him work his craft.
The soothing rhythm of it:
he tightens the mason's string, slathers cement
onto the set bricks, runs his trowel
down the middle and sets the new brick on top.
Tap-tapping it with the handle, he scoops
off the excess, indents a groove between the bricks.

Slow and steady, brick by brick, he builds—
his deft motions elegant, the click and rattle of his trowel
like a distant drumbeat—or the slow clacking of a train
along its track.

Daily Bread

Last night I dreamed I stood
at a kitchen counter full of open bread slices
staring up at me expectantly—
this after a week of making stacks of sandwiches
for hungry grandchildren.

I can see my mother standing at our old
Formica counter performing this very task.
In her self-sewn skirt and blouse after her day's work
running a school, she'd have served us
a casserole dinner and cleaned up.

She'd call out in a lilting voice, asking the five of us—
my dad grading papers, kids hunched over homework—
our preferences for the next day's lunch.
As if this was a lark.

Her slices too filled the counter as she laid them out
each pair a white prayer book ready to be composed
as she spread on the liverwurst or deviled ham
with practiced precision—just to the edges, but not over.

Then the rip of waxed paper as she began the wrapping
tucking the corners under, stuffing each into a brown bag
to be handed off the next morning
simple food with a simple blessing.

Nightly labor.
Daily bread.

Accidental Gift

I was ten and carefree and all I knew about hills
was how much fun it was to bike down
the steepest ones as fast as I could go
wind whipping wild through my hair,
plastering my clothes against me

until the day I squeezed the front brake
too hard too quickly and felt myself flying
over the handlebars, then skidding
along the blacktop to a gritty halt.

My friend caught up to me sobbing
oh kid! oh kid! oh kid! again and again
and helped me stumble home bleeding.
We plucked bits of gravel from my arm.

Days later, seeing the gauze stuck to the wound
my father came to kneel beside me
and started to peel away the silky filaments
with a small tweezers, one by one
for what seemed like an hour.

I marveled this did not hurt in the slightest
but even more at how long he knelt,
my hard-working father,
sleeves rolled up, loose tie askew
lavishing time on this delicate task

all the while giving me an unspoken message
I've carried with me through even the bleakest of days:
this is how much I was worth.

The Body as Poem

A new mother
doesn't need words
to pray. Her body
is a pulsing prayer in motion.

If there's
a part or fiber of her body
not engaged in nurturing
I don't know of it.

Transformed
from the very first moment,
no longer
merely her own,
every cell is now
for giving:

womb
        for sheltering
blood and bone marrow
        for essence
breasts
        for sustenance, solace
arms and hips
        for carrying
hands
        for tendering
heart
        for swelling to contain
        more than reason says
        it can hold.

By the Sea

I hobble a flimsy stroller along a path to the sea,
the baby bouncing in bumpy rhythm,
my daughter skipping along beside us.
Midwestern transplants we are, eager seekers.

We inhale the strangeness of this wild place,
the fishy air, the shrieks of high-spirited gulls,
the eerie clang of bell buoys,
the relentless moss-green lapping.

We scramble over sharp rocks
and dark slippery boulders to find a picnic spot.
Far off, the fog swallows boats whole as it creeps in,
a mammoth curtain of rolling gray.

Mesmerized, I assemble lunch food
on the salt-crusty outcrop we pretend is our table.
I spoon applesauce into the baby's rosebud-mouth
while I measure the size of the world.

First Hours

I wake to the sight of two small faces
perched on the mattress edge
peering intently
at the bundle between us.

On tiptoes, leaning in, my daughters
prop their chins on their soft hands
while I rest after a night of labor,
having given birth an hour ago.
The midwife is gone, the father
downstairs preparing food.

I have an important job for you two I say.
While I rest, watch your brother
(the word clearly thrills).
See how his chest moves up and down as he sleeps?
Wake me if he cries.
Like hummingbirds hovering
they monitor his every breath
his small body throbbing a steady rhythm
beneath the green terrycloth sleeper.

He is newly arrived at this strange place.
He flails his arms over and over,
opens and closes his hands—
lost in space, falling, sensing cold air,
hunger, the too-bright light
voices no longer muted, but loud, startling.

I wake. We watch,
transfixed by this:
an infant
learning to breathe.

On Simonton Road

Mid-morning on a mid-winter's day
in an old Maine farmhouse at the end of the road—
at home with my three kids.

No car in the driveway, no one due here til after bedtime.
From the kitchen window I glimpse a few icy clothespins
glistening on the line, a massive snow drift dwarfing the swing set.

I carry stacks of things back and forth, fill the washer,
hang overalls up to dry, shepherd small bodies
up and down the chilly staircase, tie shoelaces, pick things up,
put them away. I tend to broken toys and a skinned knee,
settle disputes, press a tear-stained face against my own.

I wash their marvelous dimpled hands, sprinkle cheerios
onto the high chair tray, cut bread and cheese into triangles,
apples into wedges, oranges into smiles
and scoop baby food out with a slender spoon.

After lunch we make a plan: *let's have some fun!*
We sing our best-loved songs, make purple play dough
read Obadiah the Bold, peel stubby crayons
and watch a half hour of Sesame Street.

I wedge more logs into the hissing wood stove
and wipe squished banana off the table, plotting a plan
if they nap: read, sew on a quilt I started last week.
Then what? A sudden tiredness tugs at me.
I imagine having a place to go and a way to get there.
Even bundling us up for a supply run would delight.

Mid-afternoon on a winter's day; the hinges of the barn door
creak in the wind. I stare out at the empty street,
the single tin mailbox listing slightly at the end of the driveway.

Clothesline

A basket full of damp laundry.
I reach down to lift, snap wrinkles
out of a shirt with a flick of my wrists.
I stretch the fabric out, pinch-pin
each piece up in order of length
from smallest sock to longest pant
to make it interesting, extend my time in the sun.
This soothing rhythm:
reach   snap   stretch   pin.

Small pink shirt with blueberry smudges
silky soccer jersey with sailing logo
red corduroy overalls with one buckle missing
rose print sheets, white diapers,
torn green work shirt, my favorite jeans—
the stuff of our everydayness.
reach   snap   stretch   pin.

Like a Buddhist's sand mandala
all will be dismantled in a few hours
when I unpin, shake out,
fold the fragrance of fresh into each stiff piece.

Empty basket propped on my hip
I step back to survey my work,
the heavy clothes swaying back and forth,
the lighter ones billowing on the breeze
like Tibetan flags
tugging to fly away.

Afterthought

You start to speak
and watch the dialog bubble
over your head erase
even as it fills in.

Your finest insights
are spoken but not heard
or are forgotten—
or later attributed to someone else.

Outside the circle
the ground you stand on
is only large enough for your feet
pressed together.

The trouble with watching yourself
become an afterthought
is the withering of your words,
the way they tend to vanish like vapor.

You start second-guessing
your ideas, your self.
You are a comma,
an etcetera, miscellaneous.

You start forgetting how to raise your hand
as your words grow ever smaller,
your very self becoming an afterthought
even to you.

Low Tide

Ellipses of taupe sand emerge as the sea tugs at the river
leaving watery stripes, reflections of gray clouds
and shimmery dawn light.
Gulls patrol the tidal river, gliding as they swoop
along the rippled surface, skimming, searching.

They rise in aerial exuberance
wings arced as they soar.
Surging like powerful dancers,
they scatter the others.

The elegant heron is oblivious to all this showy behavior—
the dramatic gestures, the relentless raucous cawing.
She prefers her own company, displaces no others
as she tentatively makes her way
in a rhythmic   halting   cadence.

She stops still to listen and to wait
lifting one delicate leg up
from the marshy mud each time she steps
as if unsure of her surroundings.

I too listen and wait, share her hesitation
as I witness the timeless scene unfolding.
Still, I'm drawn into this spacious sanctuary,
this exquisite dance, this knowing
pulsing through my veins
that I too belong here.

After All

Looking back on efforts that once
consumed vast amounts of energy,
it seems puzzling, the way they drove us so.
Ambitions that once filled our waking hours
have somehow lost their mighty grip on us.

Goals we depleted ourselves to reach
may have eluded us in the end:
the career derailed, the marriage collapsed
the house flooded, the business gone under.
Our labors now appear misguided.
We slap our foreheads, *what a waste*.

But maybe it wasn't about the destination
but rather the striving, the offering
the steadfast staggering toward goals—
the effort itself the point, as T.S. Eliot said.

We spend ourselves in a riot of generosity,
make our best calls from an obstructed view
and race headlong toward the vision.
Maybe it's only later we see what matters:
putting ourselves out there
merging our efforts with the energies of others
fueling the force field around us.

This might be what holds us together
makes openings for mercy
and tethers us to the planet—
Maybe it was never about the result after all.

Stitching

The very definition of boredom is how my kids now describe
spending so much of their youth in fabric stores. Somehow
they found clever ways to amuse themselves: hiding under tables
laden with bolts, flipping through zipper packets, rolling thread
spools of every color back and forth on their narrow tracks.

I got hooked on sewing early on. Irresistible, the fine lawn
of baby smocks, soft-to-touch white cotton speckled
with miniature rosebuds, Watch-plaid flannel, creamy muslin
and ridged corduroy—the sheer sensory richness of it all.

And yes, it's true there were many trips scouting for material
as I became a bit obsessed: something fun to do while housebound
something that would actually stay done,
something I could do while humming children's songs,
my foot working the pedal as toy cars rumbled over it.

I stitched cushions for wicker chairs, quilts, pillows,
miles of curtains, clothes for myself and the kids,
teddy bears, First Communion dresses, tablecloths,
dozens of napkins, shower curtains with metal grommets.
I patched knee and elbow holes, sewed hems,
buttonholes, needlepoint and cross-stitch samplers.

What was the point of all that sewing anyway?
Each day turned seamlessly into another, the way
my chugging needle curved around pockets without stopping.
Maybe I was stitching myself together
or patching what I could find into a comforter
or trying to keep us from unraveling
as if a fortress of fabric could protect us.

The Thread

A face stares out at me
from a scuffed-up photo
taken a hundred twenty years ago,
a young girl with her sisters
near a Wisconsin farm.
I stare back
startled
for her face
is the very face
of my own granddaughter.

Who is this girl? I ask,
the one on the left.
My cousin says *that's
your grandmother.*

        There is a road
        connecting the heartland
        to the East coast,
        a thread
        stitched through my mother's
        handmade clothes
        and my daughters' quilts,
        a bridge
        between my father's
        rumbling cement mixer
        and my son's law books.

        There is a current coursing
        through these two Marys—
        each on the brink of womanhood—
        who never met
        but are linked for all time.

Going Down

I could see he was down on his luck
as I crouched beside him, close enough
to take in his crumpled clothes and holey hat.
He'd just tumbled down the full length
of the steep subway escalator
and now sat folded into himself on the landing.

Small dots of blood were plunking like tears
from his forehead onto his tan knapsack.
Making futile dabs at them, I passed him tissues
while we waited for help.

I'm sorry you got hurt I said.
He mumbled, head lowered. Minutes passed.
I'm sorry   thank you   I'm sorry   thank you
we muttered back and forth, the distance between us
much thinner than we thought.

At our feet was his knapsack, packed with care this morning,
buckles neatly fastened to hold his fragile hopes
for this day, now speckled with rosy splotches.
A knapsack like that could break your heart.

Flashbacks to times when I too have lost my footing,
my plans dashed in a moment,
the memory of how it feels to be going down,
to fall so hard you cannot get up
and afterwards to weep at the brokenness.

Seeking

Where could one ever find
better news than this?
Seek and ye shall find—
especially if ye means me.
For I do seem to spend unseemly
amounts of time seeking

and wouldn't it be marvelous
to find even a fraction
of the stuff I keep losing?
Like my all-time best sneakers
(now jogging around the Costa Rican
countryside on someone else's feet)
or the words to songs my dad and I used to sing
washing dishes together
or legs happy to hike ten miles without objecting
or the threads that once connected me
with people I can't stop loving.

Not to mention the things
I don't even realize I should be seeking:
like a mystical experience of some sort
or an understanding of how whales
teach each other songs
or more advanced thinking skills
to help me grasp the laws of physics

or broader shoulders
and a core of courage
so I can finally stop fearing and fleeing
the great loneliness.

Nahant

is what Native Americans called it, meaning two things united,
because two islands connected to form this land mass
when tectonic plates shifted and lifted them up long ago.

Odds were slim we'd each be invited to a dance
in this unknown place one drizzly summer night,
decide to go despite misgivings.

My friends cancelled due to the rain, guaranteeing
I'd get lost navigating on my own. Foggy.
Maybe a good night to stay home.

But I ventured forth over dark roads
until I saw lights ahead. I sprinted through the drizzle
into the crowded hall. Nahant.

In another town, you changed plans, grabbed your grey tweed jacket
and drove to a rainy parking lot. Music pulsed out the open doors ~
the same song playing on your radio.

You paused in your circuit when a name from the past
sparked your interest. I came round to shake your hand.
You lingered. We talked. Others wandered away unnoticed.
We danced, talked deeper. Things shifted.

That night winks back at us now,
marking a place in time where two islands united.
Nahant.

Biking

Flying along the bike path this morning
I'm brushed by miniature floating kites,
the trees releasing their swirling
swatches of color with such exuberance
on this crazy-gorgeous day it makes my veins throb.

I pass a woman and beside her a young girl
furiously pedaling her tiny bike
dressed in sensible riding outfit
of helmet, fuzzy fleece and fuchsia tutu.
This too is thrilling.

The bluster of cavorting leaves
the child pedaling so earnestly
my body an orchestra of moving parts—
these call to mind the whirling dervishes,
who understood it's all about motion.

How we propel ourselves towards the light!
Not knowing where we'll end up
but swept along by great gusts of aliveness
at one with the movement of the cosmos
hurtling through space
and splintered streaks of time.

At the French Bakery

My brother loves coffee shops
so whenever he's on reprieve from the hospital
we head for one straightaway.

Today at the French bakery in Somerville
he chuckles to recount the many glitches
when he was here opening week,
the sincere wait staff in learning mode.

They're immigrant kids from blue-collar
neighborhoods—a group close to his heart—
wearing oversized white coats and hats
with shy stiffness and palpable pride.

They confer in a murmuring huddle,
courteously bungle our order several times,
then finally escort us to a table
while they straighten things out.

At last, they bring lattes and plates of pastries,
none of which we had ordered,
but which we gladly accept just before
collapsing into an eruption of laughter.

And then we cannot contain the laughter,
fountains of it bubbling up every time
we look at each other or try to get a grip
on ourselves, so that we can barely eat.

We are out of the hospital.
Charming people are trying to please us.
We are alive together, drinking coffee at a table
in a French bakery in Somerville, Massachusetts
with the sunlight streaming in.

Wandering the Halls

We wind our way down twisting corridors
my mother's small hand in mine
into elevators with masked healers in scrubs
the gravely ill attached to oxygen lines.
We are looking for my brother.
They've changed his room again.

When we find him at last, he flashes us an ashen smile.
We bring Orangina, updates from home
today's edition of the Globe.
Our dailiness floods the room.
We try to dilute his fear for just an hour,
massage our sorrow into his swollen feet.

What can we get you, we ask
as we gather ourselves to leave
promising history books next time
and the tea biscuits he loves.

We weave back through the hallways
in silence. I scan my brain
for a few words to string together
some particles of light to hold up.

We search for places inside us to hold
what we've witnessed, all we know and cannot name.
She believes I'll lead her out of this maze,
her trembling hand in mine.

*His voice is stronger today
don't you think,* I finally say.
She nods
and tightens her grip.

The Four A.M. Shift with Georgia

You burrow against my chest
tucking into yourself like a fiddlehead fern.
You're a cocoon of warm:
quiver-sighs, limb-stretches
and random shudders.

Your silky hair is dark and falls in fine fringes
over your exquisite ears.
You are fragile and feisty
timid and tenacious.

You seem confused by your sudden otherness
and the various uses of your bow-shaped mouth.
You are trying as hard as you can to get organized.
You are five days old.

Our bodies speak to each other of ageless bloodlines,
of the women who brought us here
and of the man who became a bridge connecting us.
He once nestled like you.

Morning breaks around us.
My heartbeat has begun calibrating to yours
and yours to mine,
pulsing out a promise, imprinting your identity:
beloved one.

Kinship

They share the same bloodline and spirit
separated by 97 years but sprung from the same source
always headed somewhere, full of grit and gumption.
Born to sparkle. Without even trying,
they dazzle others with their life force.

Every cell in the child is awakening, filling up
with curiosity, eagerness, wonder.
She propels herself into the world each day
built for action, bursting with energy.

Her great-grandmother too
once charged through her days, a whirlwind—
vibrant, open-hearted, luminous.
She has lived to see her children's children's children.

Now her essence is fading, dissipating day by day
whole rooms of her mind no longer occupied
the edges of her self-ness smudged and blurred—
like time, which now escapes her grasp.

Their orbits intersected, bodies touching for a brief time.
Something passed between them.
They are poster girl bookends for a long and wondrous story.
Soon they will part, their memory of each other
captured by a photo in an album and woven into their cells.

What I Brought to Provincetown

I brought my suitcase
with the Bosnia baggage tag
still tied to the side.
I brought my trusty bike
my green tattered knapsack
and my appetite for adventure.
I did not bring a compass.

I brought a longing to know what moves people,
what it's like where they live.
I brought yesterday's farewell kiss
still nestled in the warm curve of my neck.

I brought the memory of my brother who died,
who loved the other Cape and coldwater swimming,
who used to make a splashing vessel of himself
in the frigid Maine ocean, my kids giddy on his back.

I brought the Maine ocean.
I brought my kids,
their cells still firmly lodged
inside my tissues.

I brought more than I realized.

I brought a heart
where multitudes reside
and sorrows roam,
renting guest rooms.

What's Left

From her diminished stash she offers us
a couple of tree ornaments from the 50's
a small painted figurine with one hand missing
her glam ballroom dance shoes

a binderful of carefully typed family letters
my dad's scratchy blanket from his army cot
her boa and headband from Hello Dolly skits
boundless prayers, her fervent blessing.

She gives us what she has.
A virtuoso giver. It's what she does.
She used her five-foot self to gift four bodies
with bones, blood, breath, and being.

Here's the other half of my sandwich, she says.
You look chilly; want my sweater?
I can help you carry those heavy bags!
She can't help herself.

All you do for me! and here I have nothing
to give you, she laments today, arms open wide
palms up. She's Georgia O'Keefe without paints,
Mozart minus piano, a stage-less Bernhardt.

She pulls out a glossy brochure she got
in last week's mail from a charity group.
Here hon she says, holding it out,
I've been saving this for you.

Sniper Alley

they call it, which makes it sound narrow and dark,
as if sheltered by buildings. In reality, it is a main
thoroughfare, the very spine of downtown Sarajevo.
When war began and the city's supplies were cut off
it was the route people followed to fetch water
for their families, lugging containers back and forth
running and crouching, running and crouching.
Snipers nestled in surrounding mountains, circling the city
steadily shelling ancient buildings to smithereens
picking off those who dared venture forth
for food, school, medicine, a friend's birthday.

The snipers used flares at night, ensuring that no time was safe,
launching an average 330 grenades daily for four years.
For those trapped in the city, there was only the day-by-day
losing of what had once held comfort or meaning.
Hidden by stolen tanks, anxious men built a tunnel
to transport supplies, ammunition and the injured.
They dug by hand in lantern light, stooped over,
desperation clinging to the mud walls like grief.

The snipers' deadly obsession—what fueled it?
Let's imagine there were some among them
who watched small boys wander outside, their mothers asleep
and chose to let them simply play ball in the yard,
who let young couples dash home from work in safety.

Sniper Alley—the jugular vein of the still-stricken city of Sarajevo.
The story of what happened here is written everywhere
etched into the hollowed, pock-marked buildings
across a sea of 11,541 empty red chairs
and on the faces of the people, still bearing wounded witness.

Rounding the Bend
> *I live my life in widening circles*
> *that reach out across the world.*   —Rainer Maria Rilke

She's orbited through 98 years
of expanding circles.
She raced her Raleigh along routes
that looped the old neighborhood
whirled in wide arcs over marble dance floors
and kept a steady grip on the steering wheel
of our green Pontiac station wagon.
She linked herself to a chain of friends
around the country,
traveled the globe.

Then her eyesight began to fail.

Her circles are now contracting:
the perimeter of her apartment,
halos around lights,
plates of food she cannot see,
hearing aid batteries,
earrings and elevator buttons
she can only feel.
One by one her friends depart.

We move closer,
gather round.

Not Sure Why

I'm not sure why it matters
that I air the quilts outside
or perch pears in threes
on their sides to catch the light
on the chipped windowsill.

I don't know why we make our house
a hub or take time outdoors
each day to watch the sun
transform everything it touches.

I'm not sure why it matters
that we sit near a window when we eat
move in closer to the music
or plant cosmos in May

or that your first response
whenever I touch your shoulder
even when you're reading or sleeping
is to stroke my hand as if it's silk

I'm not sure why it matters,
but it does.

Close Encounters

Spotting me as you reach the threshold,
you crawl lickety-split over to my desk.
You grab my pant legs to pull yourself up to kneeling.
I set my work aside. Your upturned face has a look
of such pure pleading that resistance is unthinkable.

I hoist you up as you grip the neck of my sweater.
We move to the window in search of rabbits.
There, a few feet before us, we behold a bird so huge
that our bodies jerk back in amazement.

A wild turkey! I exclaim. *We've never seen one here before.*
You snap your head sideways to regard me, then
rivet your gaze on the bird. He is walking directly towards us.
Our breathing comes quick and shallow. Your eyebrows arch
your eyes grow wide, the muscles of your body taut.

The bird struts into the side yard like he owns it.
We rush to another window to follow him
your knees pressed into my waist, pumping.
A current zaps back and forth between us.
Your mouth is a perfect oval, your raised hands
curled into half-fists of anticipation.
You're a study in astonishment.

We rush to a third window to catch another glimpse
but this creature has his own wild agenda,
striding across the road without a backward glance.
We linger watching, utterly still, until he disappears,
our profiles angled toward the empty street.

Why I Write

I write to unfog the windshield to witness what's too essential to lose
like the sweaty-sweet grip of my grandchild's hand in mine
or the way my grandmother used to ever-so-slowly pin her hat on
while we all waited, stuffed in the Pontiac like cigars in a box.
I write to claim myself.

I write to reach into mystery and make guest rooms for sorrow
to gather my threads and stitch them into story.
I write because Sister Norbert Mary said I could
and helped me win a contest once.

I write because of Maya Angelou and Mary Magdalene,
Jo March and Joan of Arc, and because of the elegant heron
I once watched for an hour in a Maine tidal marsh.
I write because it feels like singing.

I write because my body once harbored three infants
and I got to be their mother,
because there are a thousand facets of sunlight
and because of love's unpredictable generosity. I write
because John O'Donohue was so ecstatic about that young violinist
and because of blueberries and winter berries and Vivaldi's Gloria.
I write because last fall the trees completely knocked me out.

I write because once long ago when I had a fever
my father came in from the outdoors to kneel down
and cradle my head in his large cool hands.
I write because of Nelson Mandela, Marie Curie, and Rachel Carson
and because of the way the nuns sang
lifting the roof off the college chapel.

I write because I finally found my way home from kindergarten
without having to walk by the house where the big dog lived
and because of Mary Oliver and Rumi and Julian of Norwich,
who said *all shall be well.*

I write because Mustang Sally was playing the night we met
and you smiled and said *well then, let's dance.*

I write because in the Bible, boats and baskets get filled
and wine jars too—not just to the brim, but overflowing—
and it feels right to keep track of these things.
I write because it's a mighty grace pulsing through us—
steady and astonishing,
like a heartbeat.

Beth Kress grew up in a small town outside Chicago and graduated from Northwestern University. She and her family lived in Camden, Maine before moving to the Boston area. She began writing poetry after careers in teaching and counseling. Kress is keenly interested in community, the natural world, our stories, and connections of all kinds. She values poetry for its power to create meaning and kinship. Her work has been published in the Snowy Egret, Spotlight, The Avalon Literary Review, Dreamers, and recently won The Willow Review Prize. She lives in Arlington, Massachusetts with her husband.

www.ingramcontent.com/pod-product-compliance
Lightning Source LLC
LaVergne TN
LVHW040117080426
835507LV00041B/1296